WAR AGAINST THE MIND: Learn To Take Control of Your Thoughts.

Andrew Stevens.

Table of Contents

Chapter 1: A Biblical Understanding of The Human Mind

Where do religious ideas and impulses originate from and why? With the development of novel dynamic neuroimaging methods like pet scanning, neuroscientists like David Linden and Michael Trimble are now avidly striving to provide the world with the answers. Their effort to discover in the brain a definite neurobiological foundation for religious belief exposes three current scientific assumptions about the mind of man:

the human mind is merely the higher faculty of the brain,\sthe functions of the human mind such as thinking, understanding, desiring, or judging are biologically generated and thus synonymous with the "higher" functions of the human brain, and,\sthe answers to the riddle of spirituality in the human mind lies within, not without.

Hopefully, most conservative Christians would disagree with such assumptions about the mind of man along with their associated scientific reduction of spiritual thinking (or for that matter sin, redemption, and sanctification) to evolutionary aberrations of neurochemical impulses. For the Christian, the mind is something far more than the sum of the brain's neurochemical transactions. Yet despite such a belief, why is the conservative Christian's working understanding of the human mind so astonishingly comparable to the current secular one? The Baker Theological Dictionary of the Bible describes the mind as "the component of the human person in which cognition takes place, and perception and choices to do good, evil, and the like come to expression." Dr. Zemek defines the mind of man as the seat of mentality, awareness, intellect, emotion, and volition. By contrast, the Oxford Dictionary's definition of the mind is practically the same, referring to the mind as "The seat of awareness, cognition, volition, and emotion or a pattern or manner of thinking or feeling."

The resemblance may be explained by the fact that modern Christians and secular evolutionary scientists have both decided to strictly characterize and define the mind largely in empirical terms of observable function (i.e., what the mind does) (i.e., what the mind does). The view of this writer is that a current empirical concentration on visible function is insufficient for a thorough comprehension of the human mind. Scripture's teaching on the mind of man goes much beyond visible function, separating its description of the mind from that of the contemporary world by characterizing it in terms of divine design, divine connection, and divine purpose. It does so for good cause. The world accords to the mind a key role in the identity, conduct, and destiny of man. The Bible accords to the mind a crucial role in sin, salvation, and sanctification. How one knows the mind of man directly influences how one understands and treats man's connection with his Creator. The stakes are unbelievably great. Christians can ill afford to adapt to the contemporary world, particularly in its view of the intellect of man.

THE MIND IN SCRIPTURE

How does God's word define and characterize the mentality of man? In the lack of a precise Hebrew term for the mind and with scant reference to it in the Gospels, solutions to this subject frequently depend on the apostle Paul's teaching. With the Koine Greek term for the mind, nous, being used nearly exclusively in Paul's epistles, it would first seem that a study of the mind should rely mostly on Paul's writings. However looks, as the cliché goes, may frequently be misleading.

The contemporary functional description of the mind as the seat of man's volitional and reasoning activities is typically taken from Paul's usage of the term nous. Based on Paul's words, four key functions have been used to characterize the mind:

Disposition, inner orientation, or moral attitude (Eph 4:17), **Practical reason,** i.e., moral awareness as it concretely dictates volition and behavior (Rom 7:22-25), **Understanding**, i.e., the mind as the capacity of knowing and the seat of wisdom (Phil 4:7), thought, judgment, and resolution (Rom 14:5).

However, the allusion to such functions is not unique to Paul or his usage of the term nous. The same functions are seen in the usage of the Greek and Hebrew term for heart, kardia in the NT (disposition, Lk 16:15; will, 2 Cor 9:7; understanding, Mk 7:21; resolution, Ac 11:23) and leb and lebab in the OT (disposition, Gen 6:5; will, Jer 23:20; understanding, Prv 19:8; resolve, Is 10:7). (disposition, Gen 6:5; will, Jer 23:20; understanding, Prv 19:8; resolve, Is 10:7). Furthermore, the LXX, the version of the Scriptures most known to Paul's original Hellenized and Gentile readership, also used the term nous six times as a translation for the Hebrew word leb or lebab. Paul, a man of the Scriptures and, before his conversion, a Hebrew of the Hebrews, was not formulating a unique functional theology of the mind to be understood separately from the context of the totality of Scripture. His choice of the word nous ties his readers to the vast theocentric OT anthropology of the heart, "the king of anthropological terms" and must thus be interpreted in light of this connection.

THE MIND AND HEART CONNECTION

The heart, leb/ lebab, in the OT refers to the total inner person, and is different but not separated from the soma, the bodily component of man. In its greatest definition, it is a broad entity that comprises a wide variety of functions, including but not limited to the abilities of thinking, judgment, understanding, and conscience - those that are most typically linked from the NT forward with the mind. In line with this OT concept, the LXX, imparting biblical truths to Greek-speaking Jews, considered the heart as the organ of noein – thinking, judging, comprehending, and willing (Jn 12:40; Is 6:10). From an NT viewpoint, the Greek word nous or mind signified the intellectual or cognitive part of the OT idea of the heart.

This is proven when Jesus recounts to His NT audience the first and greatest mandate of Dt 6:5, "...you must love the LORD your God with all your heart, and with all your soul, and with all your mind, and with all your might (Mk 12:30)." Everyone there, including the Scribes, received his statement as the word of God (Mk 12:33), even though His quotation included a fourth noun (mind) not found in the original Hebrew text. Far from contributing anything new to the Scriptures, Jesus' use of the word "mind" stresses a certain intellectual feature or action of the heart that is considered to be present in the original Hebrew language in Dt 6:5. As such, the mind is neither an agent nor a faculty of the physical brain, which, for the Greeks, would have been equated with the soma, but rather it is an agent or faculty of the heart as described by the OT.

THE MIND: THEOCENTRIC AND HOLISTIC

If therefore, one were to comprehend the mind in the same manner that both Jesus and Paul did, one must understand it within the framework of the anthropology of the

OT, notably the OT anthropology of the heart. In sharp contrast to the empirical compartmentalized anthropology of the modern world, the OT anthropology of the heart is a theocentric and holistic one, built upon three key presuppositions. These presuppositions drive our knowledge of the mind beyond basic function.

The first premise starts with a very basic statement, "In the beginning God..." It is God, by His will and word, who has planned and constructed the totality of man, including his heart and intellect.

The second premise is that God conceived and developed man, with all his intricacies, as a complete whole, not as a bundle of discrete components acting independently of one another.
The third premise is that God has fashioned man, including his heart and his thinking, for a special divine purpose. Ultimately the aim is to honor God by becoming a faithful

image or replica of the Sovereign Creator (Gen 1:27,28).

In light of these presuppositions, the Scripture teaches that the heart, as a reference to the total inner person, helps to explain the essential connection between God and man. It is the tabernacle of the soul, the entity of closest connection or opposition to its Creator, the location where the splendor of God lives in the life of the saints. The intellect thus, as an integral agent of the heart, participates at the deepest level of man in this connection with God. This reality is borne out in Paul's use of the word nous, where it is evident that his allusions to the mind are made in terms of this basic link between the entirety of man and God (e.g., Rom 1:28, 12:2, Phil 4:7, etc). (e.g., Rom 1:28, 12:2, Phil 4:7, etc.). He identifies the mind of man as the main reservoir of the truth of God or the falsehoods of man.

Within a comprehensive Scriptural framework, the heart never acts in isolation from the rest of man but is dynamically connected with the spirit, the soul, and the body. Scripture informs us that the heart relates to the rest of man by serving as the "mission control center" of man. The heart directs the whole of man (Prov 16:23; Isa 32:6). (Prov 16:23; Isa 32:6). The mind, then, is the faculty or agency used by the heart to do so. The whole of man, including his behavior and his physical body, is directed through the thinking, understanding, judging, and will of the mind (Col 1:21). The whole of man is transformed by the renewing of his mind (Rom 12:2). So then the brain, as part of the body or soma, is a servant of the mind and not its master. Furthermore, the nature of a man is the fruit of his heart and mind, not the fruit of his neurotransmitters or the chemical balance of his brain.

From the perspective of divine design, the purpose of the mind is perhaps most clearly demonstrated by Jesus in Mk 12:30, "... and you shall love the Lord your God with all your heart, and with all your soul, and with all your mind." The intellect, with its power to think, comprehend, weigh, and will, is a faculty that was meant to allow the man to adore His Creator and Savior in full truth. This involves equipping man with the ability to know God, through grasping His truth and by demonstrating His will (Lk 24:45; Rm 12:2). (Lk 24:45; Rm 12:2). It also involves the ability to command the entirety of man, including his conduct and his body, to serve God wisely and fruitfully as a manifestation of His truth and His love (Eph 4:23,24). It is a capacity that, by the renewing power of the Spirit, helps man to accomplish his ultimate goal - to glorify God by being like Him, following in His ways, thinking His thoughts, and loving with His love (Eph 4:23, 24), basically living in one with his sovereign Creator.

CONCLUSION

Where do religious ideas and impulses emerge from? Scripture teaches us that they come from the heart by way of the mind. However, Scripture does considerably more than merely describe the mind as the creator of ideas, impulses, choices, or conduct. Beyond function, Scripture informs us that the mind is a faculty or agency of the heart of man, a creation of God, designed to be the tabernacle of His truth and wisdom, enabling man to know and love God entirely, directing the whole of man to be one with His Creator, for the praise of His grace and the proclamation

Chapter 2: The Stronghold of The Mind

2 Corinthians 10:3-5
"For though we walk in the flesh, we do not war according to the flesh. 4 For the weapons of our fight are not carnal but powerful in God for breaking down strongholds, 5 throwing down arguments and every lofty thing that exalts itself against the knowledge of God, bringing every mind into captivity to the obedience of Christ..."

There is the story of a fighter who had been beatcn brutally in round five of a fight. His right eye was nearly closed from swelling and there was a cut across his left eye. His lip was split and his nose was fractured. When round five concluded, the bleeding boxer dropped unto his stool in his corner. His trainer jumped into the arena, sponged him out with water, and remarked, "Okay son, you're doing good. The guy hasn't put a touch on you." The boxer looked at his trainer with the one eye he could see through and said, "Well, if that other boxer hasn't laid a hand on me, you better check that referee, because someone is beating the daylights out of me."

We need to be honest about our struggles with sin. The devil is continuously trying to beat us up and we imperil ourselves when we don't admit it. Our minds must be open to honesty before God, and that provides us the potential to obtain triumph over the enemy. Denying what we are dealing with just deepens the pit into which we are slipping.

We are going to explore the concept found in 2 Corinthians 10:3-5. This affects the field of mind and knowledge. Satan utilized this form of attack when he enticed Eve and Adam to sin against God in the Garden of Eden. He convinced Eve to eat the fruit with an argument - an argument that appealed to her mental processes, not merely her inherent desire for nourishment. He first conquered the head and then the taste buds followed. Paul informs us that this war for the mind goes on in the lives of God's people even after they are saved. He informs us, however, that we can win this war because we have the appropriate weaponry to do so.

Now, let me give you some examples of how powerful the enemy is when it comes to producing thoughts that lead to death. Let's consider for a moment the drug problem in America, and the world as well. According to the National Survey on Drug Use and Health, 21.5 million Americans aged 12 and over battled substance abuse in 2014. The cost of this usage of stimulants is estimated at $200 billion in healthcare bills, criminal justice, lost workplace production, and legal expenses. With all the information that is accessible about the dreadful repercussions of using drugs, why does it continue and seems to be getting worse? In 2019 we are told that 130 persons die every day in America owing to an overdose of opioid medications (National Institute on Drug Abuse (NIDA). This organization reports that an increase in illicit drug use has soared to 30% in some areas in America in only one year!

Pornography, sexually transmitted illnesses, the dissolution of the household, child abuse, rage and aggression disorders, and many other problems, plague our nation - and even the individuals in our churches.

The reason people do incredibly stupid stuff is that the decision is not made by measuring facts but is decided through the unseen arguments that go on deep within the mind. The arguments are represented by numerous voices. Parents, professors, preachers, friends, and one's sinful nature get a word in the argument, but usually, the voice that has the greatest potential for a decision is one's nature. Since we are all sinners, that gives sin the highest chance of winning every time. There is, however, a means to win the war with the enemy of our hearts and a way to take down the strongholds the enemy has set up in our minds through time. That is what Paul is writing about in this verse.

Think about three things contained in our scripture.

THE GROUND OF THIS BATTLE

Where is the battle fought? Let's explore three aspects of every conflict between right and wrong that occurs:

i. Every conflict demands a battleground.

There is an area where the fight takes place. There has never been a battle without a pace to fight it. Right now, for example, the entire globe is gearing up for a war in "space." The president of the USA has even chosen to form a military department committed to our nation's protection that is devoted to the fight in space. The spiritual fight likewise must have a field on which it is fought.

ii. Every conflict concerns an argument of some type.

There has never been a battle without an argument of some type. Hitler thought that Germans were the elite group on earth and that the Aryan Race (Indo-European) was destined to rule the globe. He was confronted by some who said that he was a maniac and that put up a war designed to foil his murderous aims. The struggle was fought all over the world.

iii. Every war includes a person or individuals.

Wars are waged by people. Yes, the spiritual fight for the mind is waged by forces on two sides. The fight Paul spoke about in our chapter for this evening involves a person or individuals, and it involves the human intellect. You can argue that ownership of the individual mind is a prize trophy for Satan in this continual fight and war. He longs to gain ownership of your thoughts, for that leads to all you do.

So, what does Satan wants to accomplish with my thoughts and yours?
A.Capture

Satan seeks to captivate and take control of your thought process. In every conflict, there is a desire by each side to capture land and retain it. As I stated, there is an ongoing competition for control of space right now throughout the planet. America, China, and Russia are the primary participants in this rising assertiveness in space. The spiritual battle is fought for the control of the human psyche. Listen to what the Bible says about your mind:

Proverbs 23:7 reads, "For as he (a man) thinks in his heart, so is he."

The devil knows that what you think about is what you become. Your thoughts determine your activities, devotions, and objectives.

Jesus talked very plainly about this reality in Mark 7:18-22, when he showed that evil thoughts, murders, deceit, blasphemy, and adultery, among other immoral behaviors, originate out of the heart — from the mind.

Though the devil and his minions may drive you to acts done in the body that are evil and hurtful to you and others, the flesh is not where these evil things originate. It all starts in the mind, where we think and make judgments. Satan wants that upper ground in this spiritual conflict.

But, he wants more than that. He desires ...

B.Control

Remember, we are all sinners. Evil comes naturally to us because we were born in sin. So, Satan begins to work on us early and his objective is not to only capture the mind but to have full and perfect control of it.

Think about a robotic gadget. If you have the master codes or the master control, you can make a robotic gadget do whatever you wish it to do. You may configure it such that it performs what you like even if you are not there to observe it or manually oversee every action. Surely you have seen or perhaps even own one of those robotic vacuum machines. You can schedule the vacuum and it vacuums your house even when you are not home. After accomplishing its mission, it returns to the base and begins to recharge so it can serve you as its master the next time it is needed. That is what Satan wants in your life and mine. He intends to have ultimate control so that we will do exactly what he has programmed us to do at his command. Once he programs you in his ways, he doesn't have to be present every minute to get you to follow his directions - he has trained you to obey him.

Then, he gets his ultimate aim ...

C. Corruption

Satan will work such that He corrupts the mind to the extent where an individual truly thinks his or her wicked, immoral lifestyle is appropriate. We see that today in the way people speak and act in public. Their language and actions are horrible, but they don't even flinch as they act out in ways that are offensive to everyone around them. That is the devil's biggest accomplishment - full corruption of the human mind.

God intends for us to know Him and to walk in His light. He sent His Son to save us from the evil one, and Jesus died to make it happen. God understands that sinful existence is filled with suffering, pain, sorrow, guilt, and eventually death. The Lord intends for us to know life and that more abundantly. But, be convinced that the enemy hates God and wants you on his side in this conflict. So he does two things.

1. He Blinds the Sinner

Satan takes over the mind and strives in every manner imaginable to blind you to the truth. Millions of individuals, even billions, walk in the darkness of Satanic vision impairment. Jesus is called the Light of the World because He came to lead people out of the darkness and into the light.

The other day I saw a man on television who had surgery to rectify the problem that he could not discern colors. Everything in his universe was black, white, and tones of gray. The video captured the moment they removed his bandages and he opened his eyes to see colors for the first time. He open his eyes, glanced about a second, and burst into sobs. He threw his hands over his eyes and cried. His wife stood by him and grieved with him. The hues of the world had been unavailable to him, and the newness of his vision had overtaken his emotions. My friends, it is the way one feels when Jesus opens your eyes to His love and grace for the first time. It is little wonder that those who accept Jesus break down in tears. Many people describe being rescued as having their eyes opened. The world doesn't appear the same. The hues of the grass and sky are more gorgeous and glorious than ever before. Satan desires to keep people in blindness to the beauty of God's redemption and love.

Satan was so successful at one point in history to influence the thoughts of humanity that we read the following in Genesis 6:5-6, "Then the LORD saw that the wickedness of man was extensive in the earth and that every purpose of the thoughts of his heart was only evil constantly. 6 And the LORD was unhappy that He had made man on the earth, and He was grieved in His heart." Did you note that it was the "thoughts and intents" of the people that were so polluted that God sent the flood of wrath on the planet.

Please realize that Satan has been at this activity since the beginning and he knows every trick, scheme, and method for warping the mind. His purpose is to blind the lost person from ever receiving Christ as Lord and Savior.

Satan not only seeks to keep the lost in blindness …

2. He Deceives the Saved

Satan knows the power of a corrupted mind and so included in his battle plan is the attempt to mislead saved people into following the norms of their generation rather than believing and obeying what God has said in His Word. Note Matthew 22:37, where we learn that Jesus said, "...You shall love the LORD your God with all your heart, with all your soul, and with all your mind."

Our Lord chose the words, "...all your mind," because He realized the peril that the believer encounters as he or she attempts to authentically live the Christian life. You can't merely give part of your mind to the Lord. You must give your everything to Him.

One of the devil's great arguments is to convince the believer to isolate spiritual life from day-to-day life. In other words, go to church on Sunday but don't worry about that religious crap all week. Sure, read your Sunday School lesson or the Bible once in a while, but don't take it too seriously. His premise is that faith is like every other area of life - you just give it a corner of your life or intellect. He argues, "Come on, you don't watch football every day - you simply watch it on Saturday or Sunday - so, just handle your spiritual life the same way."

Today many people who claim faith in Christ have acquired many of the notions about life from the world rather than from God's Word. Even though these notions are rejected in scripture and have been shown hazardous at the worst and ineffective at the least, Christians use them in making everyday decisions. That is Satan's battle plan for your mind!

So, Satan works to keep unsaved people from seeing, hearing, and accepting the truth, and he works to keep Christians from living, embracing, and spreading the truth. The devil possesses a double-barreled shotgun to employ as a weapon for blinding the lost and befuddling the saved.

So, we've explored the Ground of this Battle, now let's consider what Paul says about ...

II. THE GATES OF THIS BATTLE

Paul speaks of the fortress or mighty gates that Satan erects to conceal the truth from the human mind. He goes on to illustrate that believers have the power through God to pull down these gates and strongholds that Satan has erected in the human mind.

I'm sure you've heard the narrative as to how enemies breached The Great Wall of China in ages past. The Great Wall has a history of almost 2,700 years and was built along the Chinese border to keep out attackers. The wall is over 13,000 miles long - which implies that the wall is almost four times as long as the distance between the Atlantic Coast of America and the Pacific Coast. That is some wall. The wall was powerful and looked indestructible, yet adversaries managed to get over and through the wall. It was easy! All they had to do was find one soldier along the wall who was vulnerable to a bribe. That was not difficult at all. They provided money to a gatekeeper who just opened the gate and allowed the invading force to stroll straight through.

Satan seeks to get into your mind by bribing you. He comes to the gate and bribes you with something you want very badly. He dangles the bribe in front of you, which is called temptation, and waits for you to want it strongly enough to give in. You can't beat Satan if you don't comprehend the strength of your mind.

Now, think with me about three types of minds - or three ways that Satan enters the gates and forms a stronghold.

A. Perverse Mind

Ephesians 4:22b, "concerning your past behavior, the old man which grows corrupt according to the deceitful lusts..."

Paul demonstrates that Satan knows the areas of your weakness because he has tempted you at those points to God and hence we fail to have the strength to fight with temptation. Unconfessed crimes makes our thoughts weaker and provides Satan even more capabilities in seducing us and driving us to revolt against God.

B. Polluted Mind

Some people have what can be called a dirty mind. That is, the mind has been affected via persistent sinful behaviors, or through drugs and alcohol. So many lives are being wrecked each day through the use of mind-altering chemicals. Damage is done in these circumstances, not merely to the brain, but the soul. Be assured that poor habits do the same thing to the mind that drugs do - habits generate pollution - like having unclean water in your drinking glass. Eventually, you will pay a significant price for neglecting to deal with these challenges.

A dirty mind can also be generated by reckless sinful action. Pornography is a perfect example. The mind can be turned unclean, contaminated, and poisoned by repeated action that is against God's intention. A fetid, vile mind is a playground for demons!

Now, let's add to the Perverse Mind and the Polluted Mind the following...

C. Passive Mind

Proverbs 4:23 urges us to guard the mind as every trouble in life starts from the mind. Keep the issues of life preserved. You can't just let your mind wander around like a nomad. Satan will place thoughts in your head if you leave the door open.

No rational individual gets out of a gorgeous, expensive car and leaves it unlocked, especially if important possessions are inside. Yet, many people keep their minds unlocked, even though every interaction, choice, and action of your life comes from your mind. We read in the Bible that Satan implanted thoughts into the head of Judas. He either left his mind open or just surrendered the key to the devil. Jesus once shouted to Peter, "Get behind me Satan!" Peter had left his mind unlocked and when Peter opened his mouth he revealed that an interloper had snuck inside. Later, it was Peter who remarked to Ananias, "...Ananias, why has Satan filled your heart to lie to the Holy Spirit and keep back part of the price of the land for yourself? (Acts 5:2)" Indeed, Satan will invade the docile mind. So, you see, you don't have to be wicked to allow Satan to get inside your thoughts. All you have to do is

act naturally - without considering what you
are doing.

Now, let's see the ...

III. THE GLORY OF THIS BATTLE

In 2 Corinthians 4:4, Paul exposes to us
traits of Satan.

**1. He is the deity (God with a tiny "g")
of this world
2. He blinds people to the fact that
they are lost and need Christ
3. He works diligently against the
spread of the Gospel of Jesus Christ.**

Yet, in all that Satan wants to do, and in all
the ways he targets the mind, we can be
victorious. What is necessary for victory?

A. Repentance

To repent means to "change the mind." It implies turning around and going on a new path. God calls to us with a calm, little voice. Imagine a toddler standing near a precipice — a tremendous cliff. His father knows that if he runs toward the child, the little one will turn to run away and plunge straight over the edge to his death. So, the father stretches out his arms and says, "Come to me. I have something for you. Come on!" All the while the father is holding out his arms. Life and death are in balance. If the child turns to run away, the goes over the edge and crashes into the rocks below. If he turns and runs to the father, he is saved. That is a picture of repentance from sin. God holds out His arms of love to you. His Son died on the cross for you. He loves you.

Repentance is an act of changing one's mind. It means to think differently. When you allow the Lord, and His Word, to rule your thoughts, you are defeating Satan and living in the light. The decision is yours. If you devote your thoughts to the deity of this word, Satan, you are doomed.

Did you know when Jesus visited the Seven Churches of Asia, as reported in Revelation, chapters 2 and 3, he asked five of them to repent? Yes, even churches can think erroneously, act poorly, and end up on the rocks of doom.

Now, everyone listening to me right now - has Satan had fun with your mind? Has he affected your thoughts? Has he affected your reactions and deeds? The necessity to have to rejuvenate your mind. We need a reboot! We need to repent.

B. Renewal

We must renew our commitment to Christ. Now, listen closely. Our minds can only be invaded when the gates are left open. We must keep our brains rejuvenated. How?

1. The Word of God

The Bible speaks about cleanliness and knowledge in 2 Corinthians 6:6. God's Word is clean and the information we need to combat the devil is in God's strength and Word. Stay in the Word of God. Plant it in your psyche. Answer Satan with God's Word - that is what Jesus did when He was tempted!

2. The Holy Spirit

God's presence in us is the Holy Spirit, and in 2 Corinthians 6:6 Paul speaks of our power in the Holy Spirit. Listen, we need to be filled with God's Spirit. In verse 7 Paul speaks of the "power of God," and you can be confident that we have that power available when we are filled with His power - the Holy Spirit – God's presence in us.

3. The Fellowship of God's People

In 2 Corinthians 6:17 Paul states, "' Come out from among them and be separate,' says the Lord." We must stay close to God's people, pray with each other, and keep one another accountable.

Conclusion

The generation in which we live is being swept away in the thinking and mindset of the god of this world — Satan. We must not join that style of thinking and action. We belong to God! Everyone who is rescued has been bought at a price. Let us this day make a new commitment of our minds, and hence our entire lives, to the Lord who offered Himself for us at Calvary.

Yes, there is someone here, no doubt, who has never turned from your sin to believe Christ as Lord and Savior. You may do that now. This is the approved time. Now is the moment. This is the day of Salvation.

Chapter 3: Winning The War Of The Mind.

The apostle Paul tells the church in Rome to not be conformed to this world, but to be converted by the renewing of their minds (Romans 12:2). (Romans 12:2). Then, in instructing the church in Corinth on how to participate in the spiritual fight around them, he tells them to take every thought captive to follow Christ (2 Corinthians 10:5). (2 Corinthians 10:5).

In a world gone wild, surrounded by the enemies of our spirit aiming to divert and ruin us, we need the truths of the gospel presented to our brains every day.

1. Challenge Your Thoughts

Have you ever slowed down to pay attention to what is going on in your mind?

What are you hearing?

What are you thinking?

What are you believing?

We are continuously being influenced by words and ideas, worldviews, and ideologies. Our personal stories are riddled with failure, brokenness, and grief. And our hearts and brains have been influenced by falsehoods, deception, and accusations from the world, the flesh, and the devil.

We need to take prisoner our ideas and study them. To capture something captive is to take control of it and place it in a controlled setting — like placing a fierce animal in a cage. Then, we need to take a critical look at our ideas and analyze what we are thinking or believing and why.

As we do this, we need to assess whether our ideas match up with what is true about Jesus and our new life in him. Does our thinking adhere to the facts of the gospel?

Ask yourself: Am I thinking or believing the good news about God, others, or myself?

The enemies of our soul spew falsehoods about God to entice us, develop mistrust in relationships to split us, and replay accusatory words in our ears to destroy us. What types of words are you hearing in your mind?

2. Bring Your Mind into Submission

As you collect ideas, encourage the Holy Spirit to bring them into subjection to Jesus – to the realities of the gospel. We have been given the Spirit to make known the truth about Jesus and to convict us of anything not in keeping with the gospel (John 14–16). (John 14–16).

Here are some of the important questions you might request the Spirit to address in you:

•Is this truly true, or is this a lie?

•Does this sound like the devil's accusation or the Spirit's conviction?

•What am I placing my faith in now: God's word or work, or someone else's?

•How do the facts of Jesus's life, death, and resurrection address this thinking or belief?

•What about Jesus do I need to remember right now?

Prayer is not merely presenting my petitions to God. Prayer is about surrendering my ideas and beliefs to God's Spirit, so that my mind may be refreshed by the truths of God's word as I submit and listen.

3. Consider the Fruit

As we yield to the testimony and guidance of the Spirit, we will also experience the fruit of the Spirit.

Paul characterizes the fruit of the Spirit in Galatians 5:22–23 as love, joy, peace, patience, kindness, goodness, faithfulness, gentleness, and self-control — a nine-dimensional life that reflects Jesus. The works of the flesh, on the other hand, produce a life contrary to Jesus's example, such as "sexual immorality, impurity, sensuality, idolatry [making a good thing a god-thing], sorcery, enmity, strife, jealousy, fits of anger, rivalries, dissensions, divisions, envy, drunkenness, orgies, and things like these" (Galatians 5:19–21). (Galatians 5:19–21).

One of the ways we battle the conflict of the mind is by evaluating the fruit we're now experiencing, or the fruit we might experience if we engaged in a specific idea or proposed action. If the fruit doesn't mirror the fruit of the Spirit or the life of Jesus, we can be assured that our thoughts are not now in surrender to Jesus. Instead, we are surrendered to someone or something else.

The Spirit gives conviction and guides us in repentance. Repentance is not only a change of conduct but a change of thought that creates altered behaviors. We need the Spirit to expose where we have believed falsehoods and to bring us to the truth about Jesus, allowing both eyes to see and hearts to trust. As the Spirit moves, we will experience a shift of attitude that will transform the way we live.

4. Fight Back

The battle of your mind is not a passive activity, but an active, aggressive conflict, conducted with the force of God and spiritual weapons made accessible to us by the gospel. As the Spirit makes the realities of Jesus known to you, you must hold on to them (1 Corinthians 15:2), take shelter in them, and learn to aggressively battle with them.

Paul admonished the church at Ephesus, "Finally, be strong in the Lord and the power of his might. Put on the entire armor of God, so you may be able to stand against the schemes of the devil" (Ephesians 6:10–11). (Ephesians 6:10–11). He then went on to outline the armor made accessible to us by the gospel (Ephesians 6:14–18). (Ephesians 6:14–18).

We conduct combat by having the realities of the gospel around us like a belt, holding everything else up. Our hearts are safeguarded by the armor of Jesus's righteousness. We have a willingness — a speed — to escape from evil and pursue compliance because we know we are free and unconstrained by guilt, shame, and fear. Because of Jesus, our guilt is gone, our humiliation is covered, and our fear is destroyed because he is triumphant over our foes.

Take up the shield of faith. Believe. Believe in what God has achieved for you in Jesus Christ. Cover your thoughts with the helmet of salvation to shield you from the falsehoods, accusations, and temptations you're destined to confront. And use the weapon you have been given, the word of God. Speak the facts of Jesus to face the assaults of the devil.

And amid all of this, continue to rely upon the Spirit in prayer. The weapons will never be adequate if you don't walk in the strength of the Spirit who empowers them all.

Take your ideas captive and study them thoroughly. Bring them into subjugation. Consider the fruit. Then fight back with gospel truths. This is how we go to war.

One of the great challenges of the Christian life is allowing Christ in to transform our mind.

•The transformed mind is the mind of Christ.
•It is the mind of the Spirit.
•It is the renewed mind.
•It is a new way of thinking and living.
•It is a mind that thinks like Christ.

What would your life be like if you thought like Jesus?

What would happen if for one week you only thought like Jesus?

Would it change your joy and peace?
Would your faith increase?
How would you feel?
Would you make any changes in what you said and did?

Would you alter your plans?
Would you treat other people differently?
Would your priorities change?
What would happen if you thought like Jesus?

Ephesians 4:20-24 NKJV But you have not so learned Christ, if indeed you have heard Him and have been taught by Him, as the truth is in Jesus: that you put off, concerning your former conduct, the old man which grows corrupt according to the deceitful lusts, and be renewed in the spirit of your mind, and that you put on the new man which was created according to God, in true righteousness and holiness.

God wants this transformation to take place in our lives.

The word transform or transformation is found three times in the New Testament.

Two different Greek words are translated transform.

The first word is used in two of the instances, (Romans 12:2; 2 Corinthians 3:18). It refers to an inner kind of change that affects our character, moral behavior, and thoughts.
The second word refers to a change in appearance or outward change, (Philippians 3:21).
God wants both of these things to happen in our lives.

These texts describe different stages of transformation.

There is a beginning, a process, and a finished product.

When we were first saved, a dramatic transformation took place in us.

We are made a new creation.

2 Corinthians 5:17 NKJV Therefore, if anyone is in Christ, he is a new creation; old things have passed away; behold, all things have become new.

When we believed on the Lord Jesus Christ and repented of our sins, we were made a new creation. The transformation began.

Romans 8:10-11 NKJV And if Christ is in you, the body is dead because of sin, but the Spirit is life because of righteousness. But if the Spirit of Him who raised Jesus from the dead dwells in you, He who raised Christ from the dead will also give life to your mortal bodies through His Spirit who dwells in you.

This is a glorious transformation from the old life to a new life in Christ. The power and guilt of sin was broken, and we were made a new creation in Christ Jesus.

Romans 12:1-2 NKJV I beseech you therefore, brethren, by the mercies of God, that you present your bodies a living sacrifice, holy, acceptable to God, which is your reasonable service. And do not be conformed to this world, but be transformed by the renewing of your mind, that you may prove what is that good and acceptable and perfect will of God.

The second stage of this transformation happens as we present our bodies and minds to God.

The text says: "Be transformed by the renewing of your mind." The mind brings about changes in behavior.

As soon as we believe and receive Christ into our hearts and lives, we are changed.

Initially, God's attitude toward us changes.
God sees us as His very own.
God counts us as His children.
Instantly we are changed from the kingdom
of darkness into the kingdom of light.
When we are saved, God fully accepts us in
Christ Jesus.
He loves us completely.
He forgives us fully.
He accepts us as His own.
He gives us new life, the life and victory of
Christ.
Our spirit, which was dead in sin, is made
alive by grace.
Our lives are set free to have fellowship with
God.
Our spirit is made alive within us.

The transforming of our mind is a process
that we must be engaged in daily.

**Ephesians 4:22-24 NLT Throw off
your old sinful nature and your**

former way of life, which is corrupted by lust and deception. Instead, let the Spirit renew your thoughts and attitudes. Put on your new nature, created to be like God—truly righteous and holy.

We are to PUT ON our "new nature." To achieve any success in this, we must first THROW OFF our old sinful nature. We will be totally unsuccessful PUTTING ON our new nature if we do not THROW OFF the old sinful nature. God wants us to have a complete transformation and not a mingling of two natures.

What is our old sinful nature?

The old sinful nature is corrupted by the power of sin. That old nature is contrary to the life of the Spirit and the life of Christ. It is grievous to the Holy Spirit for us to have a mind that is out of sync with Him. That old mind of the flesh is open to many attitudes and activities that are not in harmony with God.

After telling us to throw off the old sinful nature, the Bible tells us several things that grieve the Holy Spirit.

It mentions lying, anger, and being open to Satan's deception. It tells us to stop stealing and corrupt speech. It tells us to put away bitterness, wrath, anger, harsh words, and all types of evil behavior.

When we start this process of throwing off the old sinful nature, we must replace it with the mind and nature of Christ.

We are not stuck with who we were. We are not stuck with the corruption of our old nature. You don't have to be stuck with who you were. Jesus can change your heart and mind. He wants us to have a heart like His! He wants us to have the mind of Christ and the Spirit.

Galatians 2:20 shows how God started remodeling our heart and mind.

Galatians 2:20 NKJV I have been crucified with Christ; it is no longer I who live, but Christ lives in me; and the life which I now live in the flesh I live by faith in the Son of God, who loved me and gave Himself for me.

The process goes as fast as you will let it.

We have to give Him all our hang-ups and heart troubles. God will not take anything from us that we are not willing to throw off. It is amazing to see how quickly we can gain victory over our old nature.

The world struggles with these areas.The world tries to love. It tries to find peace and contentment. It has many break-ups and break-downs because it does not have power to make these changes.

We have something that the world does not have.

The thing that is different in us is the abiding presence and power of the Holy Spirit. As soon as you start moving in the direction the Holy Spirit is working, you will experience the victory that overcomes the world. The law of the Sprit of life in Christ Jesus makes you free from the law of sin and death, (Romans 8:1). The Holy Spirit will generate and energize your renewed spirit and mind.

The ultimate goal of God's transformation is seen in Philippians 3:21.

Philippians 3:21 NKJV The Lord Jesus Christ "will transform our lowly body that it may be conformed to His glorious body, according to the working by which He is able even to subdue all things to Himself."

This passage refers to the hope of every Christian.

One day, Jesus Christ will completely finish what he started. He will transform our bodies. Right now we are subject to failure and death. When the Lord is finished, we will be like Him. We will be changed, not only in our spirit and mind. We will be changed in mind, body and spirit.

What is already true about our spirit will THEN be reflected in our bodies.

We are not stuck with these bodies.

We are not stuck with our failures.

We are not stuck with our nastiness.

We are not stuck with our bitterness.

We are not stuck with our hurts, our pains, our illnesses, our cancers of the body and mind.

We look forward to that day when the transformation is completed.

God wants to give us a change in our minds that will impact our lives here and now.

We need to be transformed by renewing our mind, (Romans 12:1-2).

This is where the life of victory in Christ is lived.

Many believers fail in this area. They are miserable and defeated. They struggle with everyday life. Their faith and expectation for good is low. They don't know what God has done and will do for them. Their thoughts are negative and wrong. They are full of fear and doubt. Their minds are troubled and they have little peace. They are conforming to an old nature.

If you are going through any of that, you need to take immediate action.

2 Corinthians 10:5 tells us to bring every thought into captivity to the obedience of Christ.

Romans 12:1-2 tells us to not be like the world, but be transformed by the renewing of our mind.

Whenever we start demonstrating the old nature, we must stop, throw it off, and conform to the nature of Christ. We have to take decisive action in our own lives. We have to learn to adapt and line up with Christ. We have to bring our thoughts, speech, and actions into alignment with Christ.

Romans 12:2 The Philips translation says: "Do not let the world squeeze you into its own mold."

The Amplified Version says this, "Don't copy the behaviors and customs of this world."

Psalm 19:14 NKJV Let the words of my mouth and the meditation of my heart Be acceptable in Your sight, O Lord, my strength and my Redeemer.

Proverbs 2 says... "The Lord grants wisdom... He is your shield... He will guard and protect your pathway. He will cause you to make the right decision every time."

Start meditating on that.

God, You are guarding and shielding my pathway. You are leading me in the right way. You cause me to make the right decision every time.

We need to get it out of the pages of the Bible and get it into our mind.

Your mind will start lining up with the Word of God.

Repeat the Word of God to yourself.

"Greater is He that is in me than he that is in the world." (1 John 4:4)

You can overcome.

God has made a way to escape.

God has given you His Word.

You need to get it into your mind.

Don't just study it.

Meditate on it day and night.

Speak it out loud.

Allow it to change your thoughts and behavior.

Throw off the old and conform to the Word of God.

It has power to bring changes in you.

Joshua 1:8 NKJV This Book of the Law shall not depart from your mouth, but you shall meditate in it day and night, that you may observe to do according to all that is written in it. For then you will make your way prosperous, and then you will have good success.

Psalm 1:1-3 NKJV Blessed is the man who walks not in the counsel of the ungodly, nor stands in the path of sinners, nor sits in the seat of the scornful; but his delight is in the law

of the Lord, and in His law he meditates day and night. He shall be like a tree planted by the rivers of water, that brings forth its fruit in its season, whose leaf also shall not wither; and whatever he does shall prosper.